MY MAGNIFICENT HAIR

Written by
Natalee Antoinette Johnson

My Magnificent Hair by Natalee Antoinette Johnson

Publisher: In Our Words Inc. / inourwords.ca / inourwords@bell.net

Book Design: Shirley Aguinaldo

Photo Images: 123RF.com
　　　　　　　Shutterstock

Library and Archives Canada Cataloguing in Publication

Johnson, Natalee Antoinette, author
　　　My magnificent hair / Natalee Antoinette Johnson.

ISBN 978-1-926926-70-4 (paperback)

　　　1. Hairdressing of Blacks--Juvenile literature.
2. Hairdressing of African Americans--Juvenile literature.
3. Hairstyles--Social aspects--Juvenile literature. 4. Beauty, Personal--Social aspects--Juvenile literature. 5. Hairstyles--Juvenile literature. 6. Beauty, Personal--Juvenile literature.
I. Title.

GT2290.J64 2016　　　　　j391.5　　　　C2016-904497-1

All Rights Reserved. Copyright © Natalee Antoinette Johnson, 2016.
The author retains all rights to the contents of this book.
Brief quotes may be used with source credit.

To purchase books and author bookings, please contact:
info@passion4dreamsinc.com

Dedicated to:

My son JèSean, my sister Vinisha,

and all my family and extended family.

My magnificent hair
> Oh, how I love my magnificent hair
>> The different textures of my hair
>>> Oh, how I love my magnificent hair.

Oh, how I love my magnificent hair
The different textures of my hair
My natural afro looks like a halo
Oh, how I love my magnificent hair.

Oh, I love my magnificent hair
　　The different textures of my hair
　　　I love to get a fade haircut
　　　　Oh, how I love my magnificent hair.

Oh, how I love my magnificent hair
The different textures of my hair
The curls that twist round and round
Oh, how I love my magnificent hair.

Oh, how I love my magnificent hair
The different textures of my hair
The many dreads in my hair
Oh, how I love my magnificent hair.

Oh, how I love my magnificent hair
 The different textures of my hair
  I can wear it short or I can wear it long
   Oh, how I love my magnificent hair.

Oh, how I love my magnificent hair
The different textures of my hair
It looks so neat when it's set in cornrow braids
It's worth the wait because it looks so great
Oh, how I love my magnificent hair.

Oh, how I love my magnificent hair
The different textures of my hair
I can wear it in braids
Oh, how I love my magnificent hair.

Oh, how I love my magnificent hair
The different textures of my hair
I set it with beads, clips and ribbons
Oh, how I love my magnificent hair.

Oh, how I love my magnificent hair
　The different textures of my hair
　　Be it straightened or with extensions
　　　Oh, how I love my magnificent hair.

Oh, how I love my magnificent hair
The different textures of my hair
I can wear it up or I can wear it down
Oh, how I love my magnificent hair.

My magnificent hair
    Oh, how I love my magnificent hair
        The different textures of my hair
            Oh, how I love my magnificent hair.

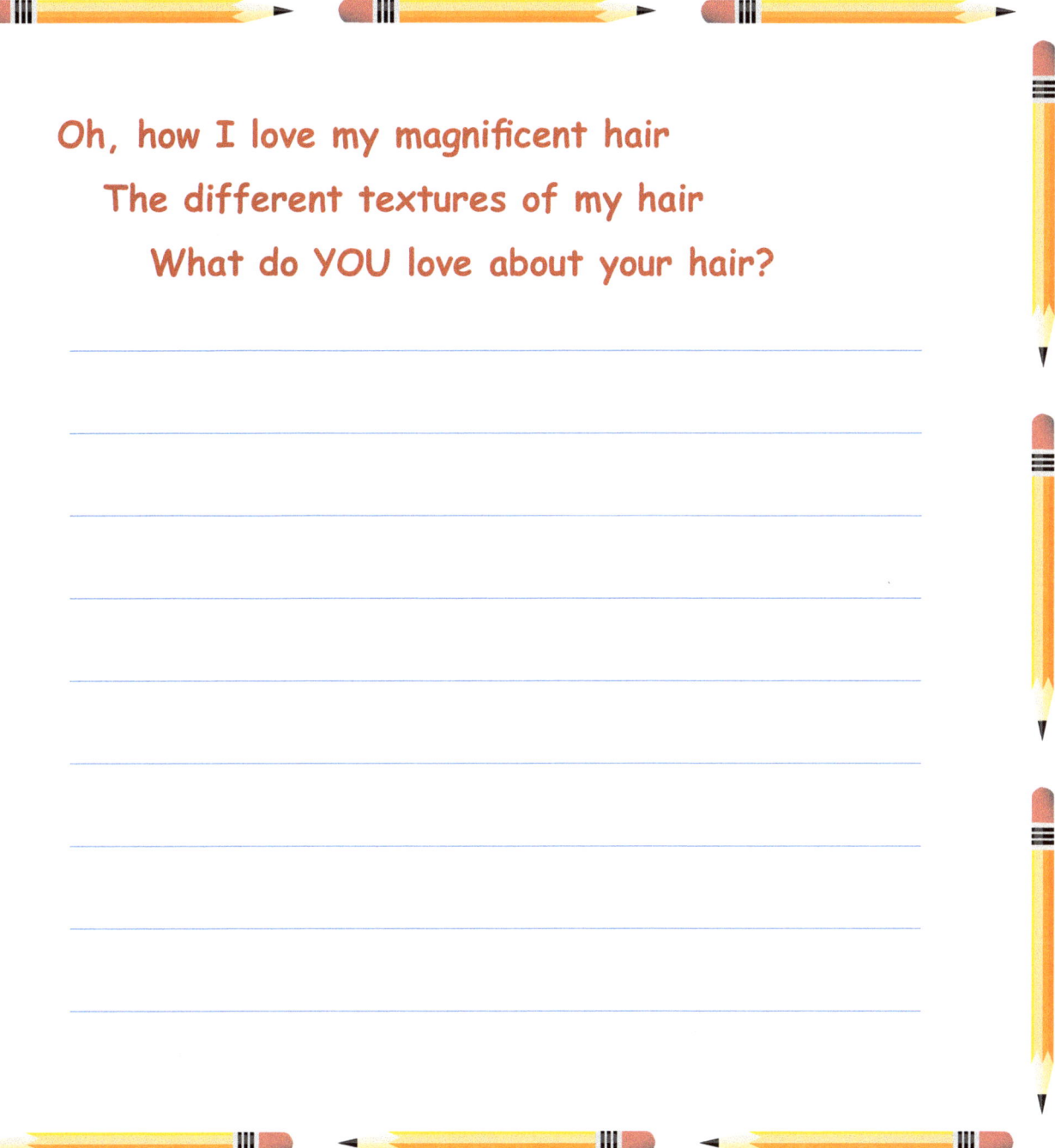

Oh, how I love my magnificent hair
The different textures of my hair
What do YOU love about your hair?

My hair story...

I remember going to school as a child with braids in my hair. Being Caribbean Canadian, my hair was different from that of many of the students in my class. When my mother washed my hair, it would curl up tightly, 'shrinking' to a much shorter length when wet. As a child, after she washed my hair, I would sit on the floor in front of her so that she could comb my hair. My mother would use the comb to part sections of my naturally thick hair and carefully braid it. Sometimes I would have ribbons, clips and beads added to my hair.

One day in elementary school, I opened up my braids and combed my hair. I wanted it to look like some of the other girls in my class who were from different cultures. As a child and youth, I didn't realize the many things I could do with my hair and the many different hairstyles I could create. My parents told me many times that my hair is beautiful. As my mom would tell my younger sister and I, "Your hair is your beauty," which meant our hair is beautiful.

As an adult, I started to embrace my thick, natural hair. I realized that my hair is magnificent with its natural curl, thick and healthy. It may be different from many others, but that's what makes it magnificent, as we all have different textures of hair. My hair is versatile, I can style it in many ways—that is, I can wear it straight, curly, braided, in twists, as an afro, or put in extensions.

'Oh, how I love my magnificent hair

The different textures of my hair.'

This book is written to encourage others, including young children within culturally diverse communities to embrace and love their hair and culture. Remember: Love who you are and everything about you!

www.ingramcontent.com/pod-product-compliance
Lightning Source LLC
Chambersburg PA
CBHW051252110526
44588CB00025B/2960